QUARANTINED

C V Williams

Synopsis: An experience of compulsory quarantine for an Australian traveller returning home during the coronavirus pandemic. Stranded in Peru when the country's borders closed early in the year, she was lucky to find a seat on a chartered plane run by an adventure tour company, after the Australian Government failed to organise a Qantas flight to bring nationals home.

First edition ebook: Sydney 2020
Publisher: Sydney School of Arts & Humanities
15-17 Argyle Place Millers Point NSW 2000

www.ssoa.com.au

Quarantined
ISBN: 978-0-6482036-0-5 (ebook)
ISBN: 978-0-9945441-7-9 (print book)

Copyright ©C V Williams, 2020

This is a work of impressionistic/creative non-fiction and any references to any actual persons are intended as benign. Cover design by Ferdinando Manzo. Typeset in Calibri. Distributed by Lightning Source.

National Library of Australia Cataloguing-in-Publication data:
C V Williams, author.
Quarantined / C V Williams ISBN 978-0-9945441-7-9

Non-fiction – memoir – life story – Australian stories – Australian current affairs

Acknowledgements

This blog, written during compulsory quarantine, was my connection to a humdrum world we all used to share but didn't appreciate.

My thanks must go to the Travelodge Hotel, Wentworth Avenue, Sydney, for the generous assistance of management and staff throughout the stay.

Special thanks to Ferdinando Manzo for encouragement to write what developed into a blog posted over the period of a fortnight, and for his assistance with publication.

I'm also grateful to all those friends and strangers who gave me encouragement and emotional succour while I was locked in that hotel room.

They made contact by phone, text and email to bolster my spirits from time to time, lessening the sense of isolation I felt. 'We are one but we are many …'

Contents

Part 1 page 9
2 Weeks in Compulsory Isolation

Part 2 page 15
Yes! I've done it!

Part 3 page 21
You know how there's always someone in your life
who 'gets on your goat'?

Part 4 page 27
Friday Night Staying In (for a change)

Part 5 page 33
Wasn't it superb to have a sunny Sunday to relax?

Part 6 page 39
One week down – one to go!

Part 7 page 45
Let me begin today with a joke since they're scarce these days …

Part 8 page 53
Feeling rather house proud today

Part 9 page 57
As one of the travellers from Peru quarantined …

Part 10 page 65
Ooh-la-la Easter Monday

Part 1
2 Weeks in Compulsory Isolation

I've been pondering the amount of time & effort I put into planning for about half a year a trip to Peru, only to find myself in a small hotel room in Sydney, wishing I could open a window. Lack of fresh air seems to be the main complaint from people being restrained in our city hotel. Or so I'm told by Andrew, the friendly police-person at hotel reception, so well-trained in PR.

Having taken a cheap flight to Peru in early March, I managed to stay in Lima for 3 weeks before taking the first expensive commercial 'repatriation' flight out to Sydney on Sunday, March 29. The flight organised by Chimu Adventures and flown by Chile's Latam airline, was recommended by the Australian Embassy in Peru.

(Postscript: The Australian Ambassdor in Peru has just this morning - April 1, Australian time - put out a call for all Australians in Peru who want to return home to register for a possible second flight by sending their details to consular.lima@dfat.gov.au).

I'd had one fabulous outing - I'd visited Larco, a museum specialising in erotic art exhibits and one of the most beautiful restaurants in the world. Surrounded by enormous banks of crimson, orange and white bougainvillia, I was thrilled to be able to sample a classic dish, causa, made from a smooth creamy yellow potato, the country's national pride. Along with a chocolate mousse to die for. I only hope I won't have to.

After that delight it was down to the business of getting in stores before the official military lockdown, Peru's approach to protection from the spread of coronavirus, which was still showing very low numbers of people infected. Empty shelves in some supermarkets, just like in Australia, included where toilet paper used to be, and even a run on bananas.

What was different than in Australia were the impressive early declarations by the President who showed his concern to buy in thousands of extra COVID-19 test kits and insist that people could not congregate nor even drive without a special permit to do so. Our household was in serious lockdown, rubbing down with alcohol any package delivered and insisting that you were either 100% in or 100% out - there'd be no going back and forward to work every day. This lockdown was for the duration - at least for the first 15 days announced, but who knew how long an extension might last? Would I get back to family in Australia before Christmas? More detail on the negotiations to get a ride back home in a later blog ...

This week, after reading reports that some other returnees to Sydney, 'inmates' shall we call ourselves, had been put up in Sydney's poshest inns and treated like princesses, I thought I'd feel more like a model on assignment. Not prepared to get out of bed for less than $1000 (or is that $1000 an hour?), focussed on pampering my skin with moisturisers and unguents, and alert to any flaw that might appear on my toenails' 'Ruby Tuesday' glossy surface.

Well, that may still happen - but all that's occurred so far is that I've been run off my fingertips replying to friends' messages of concern, and slept through the afternoon and then the evening news from jetlag before getting a second knock on the door. This time it was for the presentation of a cold, light salad dinner in a pristine brown paper bag. As a vegetarian, I'd knocked back a chicken sandwich for lunch and was later given a salad replacement. You've got to give a little leeway, I say.

What I do think has been my greatest revelation is a slight feeling of uneasiness, a fear about not making it back home, the smallest measure of that horrific feeling that most refugees must feel: the state of homelessness. Can you imagine what horror it would be to have to tramp hundreds of kilometres with your children to the very uncertain safety of another nation, the experience of a Rohingya mother in a Bangladeshi refugee camp, or a gentle, well-educated young Iranian who finds herself on Manus Island? With no prospect of release ...

I felt just a twinge of guilt when it was announced, as our flight was about to take off for home, that two people had been rejected by the Australian Government for travel. Australia didn't want them. What, are they criminals, or suspected criminals, I wondered? I don't have any answers in this hotel room. I hope someone outside can find out ...

Tomorrow's instalment: a fond look back at the plane ride home ... and anything else of note that might be happening in my mini temporary home on the 9th floor.

Part 2
Yes! I've done it!

I was wondering how long it would take me to give up getting into day clothes, since I'm not allowed to receive visitors to my hotel room nor go out at all in this state of penitent quarantine for returned globe-trotters. So what's the point of dressing, I had to ask myself?

Then I woke this morning feeling a little rebellious. I took one look at my day dress (my daughter calls it my mini-dress but it's just above my knees, not upper thigh length, let me assure you) and I decided today was the day for 'deshabille'.

And since we've slipped so easily into French, may I use the word 'negligee'? Yes, I stayed in my neg long after I should have become respectable. At least two thirds of the day ... (And please don't act shocked that I'm not naked in bed every night. That was so 80s - and I am over forty, after all!)

The fact is my only incentive for finally deciding - by mid-afternoon - that I should dress (ie 'dress myself up') was when I had the thought that if my hand happened to slip from the door handle when I stepped outside into the hotel corridor to pick up the paper bag containing one of my meals, and the door closed behind me, I would have to go down to reception in that same state of deshabille since I'm not allowed to knock on any of my compatriots' doors. A sobering thought! So I quickly took off my 'oh so comfy between the sheets' outfit for a sensible skirt - and kissed goodbye (or do I mean 'au revoir'?) to my thoughts of a couple of quick day naps to allay the jetlag.

So, basically, I've been battling against the sweet solace of slumber to give you my impressions of the repatriation flight, as I'd promised yesterday.

It began when the Australian Embassy in Lima referred me to a travel company, Chimu Adventures, trying to organise a flight home for Australians left high and dry when Peru closed its borders at short notice - as it had every right to do for the protection of its own citizens. Some Aussies were left as high as Machu Picchu (that's over 2400 metres) and others scrambling around or queued cheek by jowl (instead of 1.5 -2 metres apart) at Lima airport.

The Ambassador was very compassionate and efficient, especially considering the circumstances, in that the Australian Federal Government had not despatched a government-authorised Qantas flight to pick up Australians abroad as it had done during the China corona outbreak. The Ambassador assisted where she could, and that was essentially to work with Chimu, DFAT, the Latam airline which runs a regular service in conjunction with Qantas to Peru via Chile, and the Chilean and Peruvian aviation authorities. No easy task, I imagine. And so there were several possible go-aheads and then delays ... until a flight finally left for Australia on Sunday March 29.

The plan had been to carry 260 Australians and New Zealanders, but with the announcements of Australian borders closed and then compulsory quarantine in Sydney, the NZers were hived off to another flight. So the numbers varied a little over the last 24 hours before take-off.

And then there was a surprise package just as we boarded the flight at the national Fuerza Aerea del Peru airforce base in Lima. Airline stewards tried to put us all in Economy despite some passengers having paid twice the price for Business class. That is, $10,800 from Lima or, from what I heard screamed out loud on board, $12,000 from Cusco. The justification given by stewards seemed to be that the first two rows (12 seats) in the Dreamliner needed to be left empty in case of a need for isolation. That is, for actual corona virus cases. Yet Chimu had told us that anyone with the infectious illness would not be allowed on board but treated in Peru. And there were another 3 rows (18 seats) which hadn't been set aside - and quite a number of those who'd paid the higher Business rate were justifiably angry that they were being shut out. 'Bullshit' was a frequent and noisy response to the arrangement and to the lame position adopted by the stewards that dissatisfied customers could claim a refund later. Needless to say some passengers prevailed, most with legitimate health concerns. But the unhappy divisive situation was repeated to some extent after the 5-and-a-half hour wait in Santiago for refuelling. Sympathy for all concerned was the only suitable response, with passengers having been stressed for weeks and then desperate for a safe way back home, while airline staff, on the frontline of dealing with the public and the possibility of contracting the illness, not fully informed of the details of the flight conditions that passengers had agreed to and paid for.

It was also disappointing to note that there were no medical checks of passengers as expected either in Lima or in Sydney, apart from a flick of the wrist temperature test near the forehead or in the ear.

Who would want that angry on-board situation repeated?

The Federal Government should get its citizens out of South America and other major centres of the world as quickly and efficiently as possible. The way Qantas has been managed over recent years, it's clearly not our national airline. The Federal Government needs a 51% stake in its ownership, not just a handover of millions of $$$$$ (at least) to add to the complexity of the company's former corporate profits and now corporate woes. This is not just a time for governments to prop up enterprises but to have them actually working in the interests of Australians.

And with that very disagreeable experience of the trip home relived in the telling (yet for which I'm still very grateful on arrival), I'm now going back to sleep, nightie in hand. (Yes, I think we're familiar enough with each other now to drop the French.)

Check you tomorrow for Day 3 in my hidey-hole.

Part 3
You know how there's always someone in your life who 'gets on your goat'?

It's not a situation peculiar to being locked up in detention. Everyone knows the feeling - someone who's a sour grapes, a spoilsport, an aggravating yin to your ebullient yang, who always knows what's best for you and doesn't hold back from nagging you constantly about it.

Well, here in my hidey-hole that annoying presence is the air-conditioning. Let's call him AC (why I've gendered his powers as male when yin is usually associated with the female, I can't imagine!).

You might remember I referred to AC in my first blog. He was blowy and wouldn't tone down his rant, while remaining far too cool. And if I went to the trouble of heating him up, firing up his ardent passion to, say, 23 or even a shocking 25 degrees, he'd seem to go along with it for an hour or two but then resume his coolness, a consistent 21.5, citing energy savings. And during the night he was positively frigid. But it was the extreme exhibitionism of his blow-hard, pushy forcefield, even on 'low fan', that made him unbearable and me nauseous.

Well, I'm not sure if it was his bellicose character or the first hot cooked meal I'd received since arriving - a stale Thai tofu dish - or, more likely, the mix of these two that created conditions that were not at all soothing to my nature - and I woke at 1.30 am with a severe headache.

Forsaking a patience I'd been trying to nurture over a couple of days, I moved straight into action.

I promptly turned off AC and propped open the door to the hotel corridor for the rest of the night, devising a method of using a piece of cutlery balanced in such a way as to prevent entry by any person, yet allowing in some corridor air.

Yes, it was also AC air, I know, but not as intense or dusty, perhaps, as AC's own personal outpourings in my private 'petite chambre'. Admittedly, I knew I would still be under the influence of AC, or one of his kind, though it would not be so intense as being force-fed by him in my small room.

Then I went to the bathroom, drank copious amounts of water and swallowed 2 Vit C tablets. Back to sleep - and I woke around 7 am, still feeling tender-headed; but come late-morning, my body was beginning to feel much more like my own.

And breakfast, a breakfast arrived like so many others I'd enjoyed in the past, and so unlike the tidbits I'd had over the previous two days. Clearly, hotel management had responded to my complaints from the day before ... even while the staff were also doing their best to satisfy the whims and fancies of so many other detainee guests.

I found out that the establishment had been required, with just 2 days warning from the government, to re open quick smart to be ship-shape ready for a band of adventurers back from South America.

There it was, this remarkable and much appreciated breakfast of yoghurt, cereal & fruit; not the inevitable chunks of melon, cut prior into pieces by unknown possibly-corona-infected hands (as I imagined) but whole fruit I could peel or cut myself! Strawberries, a banana, luscious grapes, a tempting apple and a cute nashi pear. Life had improved so markedly in just a few hours!!!

I spoke with the powers that be later in the day and finally a compromise interim measure was taken to ameliorate the situation, let's say.

I mean, too much detail about such measures is often more than a reader is able to take in. So let's just leave it there with a happy ending for this particularly inventive 3rd day of my quarantine, and conclude with news of:

1. my chat with the hotel's resident doctor reassuring me it was unlikely I was suffering coronavirus - no fever or dry cough - and ...

2. another two hot vegetarian meals: a late lunch of potato and leek soup with typically Sydney, warm artisanal bread rolls, followed by dinner of mushroom risotto.

And so it was, a heady adventure that made me feel I was safe, back home in Sydney's 'can-do/fix-it' emotional landscape, even while not yet ensconced in my own personal home sweet home. A way to go still ... 11 days, in fact.

A relief that a bunch of Australians who were stuck in Nepal have arrived back in Queensland - but what about Australians still in Peru and other parts of the world remote from their home country?

Come on Foreign Minister Payne - why so timid, neglecting your responsibilities?

Talk tomorrow - Day 4.

Part 4
Friday Night Staying In (for a change)

Plenty of time to contemplate the question of quarantine, detention, compulsory restraint or imprisonment here in this hotel room.

Yes, everyone has stayed in a hotel room, and maybe felt a bit stir crazy at times – in the middle of the night maybe, or when the weather is bad. It can even happen at home, especially if you're in an apartment without a balcony and don't have a back yard.

But the only really comparable compulsory restraint is being in gaol, which must be of a completely different dimension. Of course that would be so, so, so much worse. It's normally for much longer than 2 weeks ... stretching to years, and in rare cases close to a lifetime.

My brief quarantine experience does, though, engender a sympathy for those who are imprisoned, committed for a crime carried out either by accident or intent. And especially for those people who might have been jailed after conviction on drug charges, especially for a drug that might soon be legalised in some parts of Australia.

On arrival at this hotel the other day, the policeman who brought me up to my room in the lift gave me a bit of advice.

'Maybe it's not a good idea to tick off each day from the start. It might seem a lot longer that way. Try to relax into it, not keep counting down the days,' he said.

Not a bad idea, I thought. I'd consider the amount of time I had to relax … But no sooner did I set myself up, than I launched into a daily blog … counting the days. Duh!

Anyway, it's been a successful way to receive a great deal of goodwill, from friends and strangers alike, which I've found has been keeping me buoyant emotionally.
And I bear in mind the individuals and families who are also self-isolating, not through forced locking up, but through sheer self-discipline and a sense of solidarity to maintain a practice which will help to keep the coronavirus from spreading out of control. From a sense of community well-being. They're admirable!

Most days I don't see too many people. Now there's an understatement … Today was different. I had a couple of workers visit to adjust my window. One cleaned my aircon and also ran a vacuum cleaner over my carpet. They were very solicitous, apologising for interrupting me, concerned that I was holed up for a fortnight. I was touched.

'No problem. Take as long as you like,' I told them. 'I'm in no hurry to go anywhere or do anything.'

I also met Joan in the corridor and we had a chat that lasted about 20 seconds. I peered at her from my doorway, the door opened only for me to pick up my meal. I hadn't noticed her earlier, I guess that's because every time I poked my head out to pick up my meal, packaged in a brown paper bag, she must have been down the other end of the corridor. Joan is one of the security staff posted on every floor that holds the hotel's quarantined inmates. How many floors that is, I don't know. I found out she works the 7 am – 7.30 pm shift. Long hours! And what does she do in the job? She walks back and forth along that corridor, back and forth, back and forth; it doesn't do to walk too fast; it's pretty tough on the feet. This quarantine is a lot harder for Joan than for me, I decided. I have a TV screen, a mobile phone screen and even, since this morning, a laptop screen (we're each allowed to receive one parcel a day). Plus books to read. Who could be bored with that plethora of media access? So Joan has a harder task than me – except that she's here voluntarily, she's being paid, and she gets the privilege of being truly out in the world every morning and night, out in reality rather than in my enforced cocoon of virtual reality.

Those brown paper bags are building up. Seems such a waste to throw them out – good paper. I've begun an artwork, for contemplation on the good fortune that I am being housed, ministered to, plied with food. It's not what I'd call high art – I haven't reached the creative stage yet - haha - just another form of ticking off the days to be spent in quarantine, I guess. I wonder how the bags can be reused, since who knows whether they might carry droplets of coronavirus? I'm suspicious of every type of material these days, trying to memorise how long droplets stay on whichever material is presented to me. I learned to take note in Peru, to slow down enough to consider whether to touch something or not, to get more control over my hands.

I'm still receiving epistles from Peruvian culture. Yesterday the President stated [as translated], 'Our first priority will always be to protect the life and health of the people. Economy comes after. … We are ready to support economic reactivation boldly as soon as the virus is contained.'

As there was a 'light' earthquake in Peru yesterday, he proposed that people at home 'review their emergency backpacks and earthquake protocols'. Can you imagine the staunch bravery of the Peruvian people facing the possibility of an earthquake as well as the pandemic? I have great respect for them, thinking back to just last week when I was in Lima. Every night residents would stand on their balconies or at their front doors at 8 pm to join in clapping, in appreciation for their doctors, nurses, and all ancillary, including cleaning, staff. As the evening sky darkened, moving towards winter …

All over the world now, people of different cultures are honouring their medical staff, including volunteers, and even their teachers and childcarers, their cleaners, their garbage collectors - those people who have been at the bottom of the social rung, people we now realise we are all dependent on. Not before time! So many of us here, 'doing time' in this hotel, must think about how lucky we've been to travel the globe and return safe and sound. So far so good, in that no coronavirus symptoms have been detected in anyone in the hotel up until this point.

Sorry this update is being sent out so late today … but my internet connection has been laughably poor last night and this morning. But thanks to the calm persistent efforts of Brad at Superloop, I'm back online and in grateful mode.

On that note, I've decided to take a break from the diary blog tomorrow – Sunday, a day of rest, of recovery, of kindness and care.

Part 5
Wasn't it superb to have a sunny Sunday to relax?

Although I couldn't get out in that sunshine, I was so pleased to see it – and to see others on their balconies reading, relaxing, and even one, presumably, father and son playing catch. The boy was about 4, and it didn't take long before the father put a bit of a twist into his throw to advance beyond the loop-the-loopiness of his son's ball skills, I noticed.

I had an eventful day food-wise. I woke up starving, and realised I hadn't had any protein for days, apart from some teensy yoghurts for breakfast a couple of times, plus some milk on my cereal, so I decided to complain. Oh, those whingeing Australians, staying in fancy hotels! I know ...

In my defence, this is a 3 and a half star hotel and I've been pretty reasonable, I think – but as a vegetarian, it doesn't mean you don't want to eat foods that actually satisfy your appetite. And that's what protein does. So I rang Reception.

'You know, when I filled in the questionnaire on arrival, I ticked vegetarian (not vegan) for meals and added that I eat eggs and dairy foods,' I explained. 'I haven't had one egg since I've been here. And what about a bit of cheese sometime?'

'Well, no one else is getting eggs and cheese,' was the smart comeback.

'Yes, but they are getting some meat, aren't they?'

It made me wonder … We're unable to consort with others in a similar position, since none of us can leave our rooms. We're allowed to pop out our heads to gaze down the corridor, waiting for our food bags at meal time, but don't dare take a step out. I have no idea what the other over-400 guests in the building are eating, since they're mostly not vegetarians, I presume.

We're each allowed one personal parcel delivery a day, so many are by now ordering in, I guess. And in such a confined space it's hard not to think about when the next meal delivery will roll around, as it varies, and what surprises lie in store.

Well, breakfast arrived and there was a creamy yoghurt included. Then a lunch of not 1, but 2 boiled eggs! By mid-afternoon I had dinner delivered, an Indian chick pea curry. Plenty of protein in that lot. So it's reassuring that my complaint brought results. I may not have to complain again at any time over the next 8 days – if the message sticks.

I've heard that the Government at first offered caterers $60 per person per day for provision of meals, but reduced that to $20 – which would make it difficult for a business to employ staff and make any profit without skimping. But that might be hearsay – don't quote me on that. It would be useful for a journalist to follow up the facts though – if there are still any journalists lucky enough to have jobs …

One thing I am feeling a little perturbed about is a quality of ostracism that floats in the air whenever I have any slight interaction with meal delivery staff. They're kitted out with mask and gloves and I am too, sometimes, though I have to admit not always, since I often hear the knock on the door and jump up to answer, forgetting to don my mask – plus nothing is passed hand to hand, and we're never closer than the 2 metres rule. The food bag is left on the floor outside my door, and the deliverer has often rushed away already. But if they're still there, waiting for me, I'm treated as if I do have coronavirus.

And maybe I treat the deliverer with equal suspicion. The person might be a carrier of more than the meal; the bag may have been touched by someone with the virus, I think. It's all very unsettling in terms of human interaction and goodwill.

I've been observing the ground rules for weeks, including in Peru. Yet I feel I'm being equated with an actual sufferer from the illness. What's to be done? Cop it, I tell myself. But I think it would be a lot more helpful if we could all have a test to be ruled in or out.

Surely the temperature test would only identify the high temperature phase of the illness. Or is a high temperature in all stages? Are there simply not enough test kits available? Maybe a medical professional could answer that question for us all ...

During the afternoon I did a spot of reading – fiction, that is, as a relief from the relentless coverage of the spread of coronavirus, essential though it is to keep up with the news. I came across a piece of writing by Ivan Turgenev, just a snippet described as a 'prose poem', though I doubt he would have classified it as such. The account is titled, 'The End of the World - A Dream' – and so it seemed to be. It carried such foreboding, set in Russia: 'in the wilds ... in a room big and low-pitched with three windows; a grey monotonous sky hangs over it'. By contrast, I read it on a balmy afternoon in Sydney, aware that we're now all living through not necessarily the end of the world, but certainly as we've known it.

'I am not alone; there are some ten persons in the room with me. All quite plain people, simply dressed. They walk up and down in silence, as it were stealthily. They avoid one another, and yet are continually looking anxiously at one another.
Not one knows why he has come into this house and what people there are with him. On all the faces uneasiness and despondency ... all in turn approach the windows and look about intently as though expecting something from without.
Then again they fall to wandering up and down. Among us is a small-sized boy; from time to time he whimpers in the same thin voice, 'Father, I'm frightened!' My heart turns sick at his whimper, and I too begin to be afraid ... of what? I don't know myself. Only I feel, there is coming nearer and nearer a great, great calamity. ...'

Turgenev gave us the ending we all hope for: 'Scarcely breathing, I awoke.'

The sketch was written in March 1878, the month a treaty was signed between the Russian and Ottoman (Turkish) empires after a long and bloody war. Perhaps it is appropriate to remember now that the human race has long survived - many bitter wars, famine, pestilence and epidemics – and at this point in our history we can only look to medical science, self-discipline and bravery by the masses across the globe, to fight this latest war, a pandemic on a scale never before realised.

Note to self-interested me: I'll drop all the testy references to food in the rest of my blogs.

Copyright: Wise old owl drawing sent to me in isolation by Sydney School of Arts & Humanities member, Jennifer Neil. Sunflower photo sent by Gerdette Rooney. Turgenev quote from 'The Penguin Book of the Prose Poem', Penguin, UK, 2018, pp. 392-94.

Part 6
One week down – one to go!

As if by magic, the question I raised in my last blog about what can be learnt about the specific qualities of a virus from a test, was dealt with in an ABC interview today. It was something that had been troubling me ever since the early news of the coronavirus … and troubling most other people too, I guess, but not answered in news coverage.

HOW DOES A PERSON KNOW IF THEY'VE HAD A SLIGHT CASE, MAY STILL BE A CARRIER, MAY GET CORONAVIRUS A SECOND TIME ETC …? The questions surrounding testing of this virus are almost endless.

When I arrived in Peru on March 7, I was concerned that I'd had a sniffle and other signs of a slight cold/virus back in Sydney in Jan-Feb. Was it even possible for coronavirus to be present in Australia back then? I'm not saying my fear was rational; I'm saying we all experience some fear of infecting others. Then when someone in my family was tested and cleared as negative, I was relieved to know that I must not have been a carrier. And I'm fairly sure I haven't had any contact with the infection since.

But isn't this the KIND OF WORRY WE ALL CARRY to some degree? 'What about the time when … ?' 'I might have … ?' 'I was concerned about coming within the 1.5 – 2 metre limit the other day when …'

Today I heard about the work of Associate Professor Menno Van Zelm and his medical research colleagues at Monash University and The Alfred Hospital, and immediately felt grateful that these questions about the nature of the virus that need to be answered are the subject of specific research - along with effective treatment, and a long-term preventative vaccine being carried out elsewhere.

The ABC reported that the researchers have created a rapid test to determine a person's immunity to COVID-19 and how severe their symptoms might be.
Monash University's Menno van Zelm said it would play a crucial role in helping infected healthcare workers return to the frontline.

'Hopefully with such a test, we can determine early who is immune to the virus and can get back to work.'

The same-day blood test, similar to that for influenza, looks for immune system cells, known as memory cells, which make antibodies to fight against viruses … to be able to predict who will get a mild version of the disease and who may need care in ICU.

'We really want to employ it to understand what is different between patients with a really mild form of disease versus a severe form of disease.'
The test is still undergoing trials, but Associate Professor van Zelm believes that with sufficient funding it could be rolled out widely within months. https://www.abc.net.au/news/2020-04-06/victoria-coronavirus-death-toll-rises-as-cases-increase/12124156

So although the statistics in some parts of the world are exceedingly grim, in Australia we have taken some action (is it enough?) to flatten the curve, and the public at large does now seem to be taking the self-isolation measures seriously. There is a lot of doom and gloom – horrific images – families grieving from the onslaught of the virus. Still, there's hope in the fact that dedicated medical researchers and carers are racing against time to find answers and provide compassion where they can.

A second flight out of Peru was announced yesterday, Monday April 6 – but it won't be able to carry everyone wanting to come home. So many will have to register on the waiting list and get by however they can until arrangements are put in place for a further flight. And not only in Peru. India, Cambodia ... Australians have been great travellers for decades.

Why, oh why, couldn't the government have stepped in to bring back its citizens sooner? They hadn't left Australia after a curfew or border closure. DFAT's Smartraveller hadn't warned them against travelling at the time they left.
I feel blessed that I had the means to act early to fly back and, as I'm due to get out of quarantine next Monday good health prevailing, I hope I'll soon be returned to the reassuring fold of my homeland.

Image Unsplash - Daniel Morton

Part 7
Let me begin today with a joke since they're scarce these days …

A Canadian teacher, a Scottish pilot and a Puerta Rican lawyer walk into a bar …

They are all female. They sit 1.5 metres apart.

One asks for a drink and the other two decline her offer of a shout. Why?

Answer: the teacher is deaf, the pilot is blind, and the lawyer speaks in legalese.

Yes, there's been a bit of pressure from my being stuck in a hotel room (and never once the bar) for a week – but I'm hoping I've remained sane ... Hoping for personal reasons, you'd understand, but also because it's a guinea pig situation and since everyone is now in some degree of isolation, I'd hate to think that many people were suffering mentally from the amount of uncertainty that pervades the governmental measures that are being taken to combat coronavirus.

So – here I am trying to mix a bit of humour with a serious and complex social crisis. What I would like to do, just as a test of my clarity of thinking, is to point out what I see as a series of examples of muddled thinking by a few leading political and social leaders. And to find out whether you think I've lost it, or there is a whole lot of confused or even contradictory thinking and talking going on out there ...

1. Remember back when we were asked to get in some stores because the pandemic might last months and we might need them? It wasn't long before we were being chastised for hoarding, being told we were 'un-Australian'! Sure, you can go too far – and hiring a bus to take you to a country town to buy up all their scarce groceries was a disgrace. No question. Now I'm just hoping we can all find a happy medium in buying enough stocks to see us through hard times ahead.

2. Masks – first it was recommended we buy them, along with gloves and hand sanitiser, then they were sold out in supermarkets and pharmacies, and health workers were short of these essential items. And I do believe they are essential in caring for coronavirus patients. Then, within a week or two, we were being told that they weren't useful, and even possibly dangerous if we handled them too much. Finally, despite a statement from the World Health Or-

ganisation, controversy on the subject remains.

When it comes down to it, we all have to be careful about where we put our hands: on goods, on mobiles, on other people and on our own faces. And careful about how close we come to others or allow others to come to us, and that's certainly not close enough to breathe on strangers or even loved ones, in many cases. It takes a serious approach to social interaction, so let's leave out the judgements about whether it's right or wrong to wear masks and gloves. People are trying to do their best, I hope.

3. Then the issue of holding your children back from attending school arose. Yes, leave all schools open and send your children to school we were told by the Federal and NSW governments (even though there have now been deaths of children, not just adults, from coronavirus). At least the Victorian Premier took a hard-line approach and announced a clear-cut policy of closing all schools for first term, and only now is encouraging most children to learn from home once second term begins if they have online capability, and only go to school if it's absolutely necessary.

4. Which brings me to another mixed message – childcare. Childcare centres are staying open – and will be free for most children to attend. Now, if that isn't an incentive to send your child to childcare, I don't know what is. Except your children are the most precious people in your lives … and how would you feel if your child became infected by playing with just one other child, or by a teacher who needed to pacify your child at any moment of the day?

5. And coronavirus testing kits – how extensively are they really being used? What percentage of the population is tested daily? And is it too much to expect that a significant number of people need to

be tested? It's reported that to date over 178,000 COVID-19 tests have been carried out in Australia and that number is 'growing rapidly by the day'. The Federal Government says this testing rate – at approximately 557 tests per 100,000 people – is among the highest in the world. But what does that mean, 'among the highest'? Sometimes the word 'among' is even dropped from the description. Germany, with a population of just under 83 million, has an impressive testing record. Their scientists were able to calculate more accurately the effects of COVID-19 when testing was rolled out extensively - that is, around a million Germans were likely to become infected, and approximately 12,000 die, based on an increase in testing to 100,000 per day, and within weeks to 200,000 a day. We're not within coo-ee of that testing figure.

6. Further, what do the Prime Minister's statements about paying or not paying domestic or commercial rents mean? Property owners and tenants have been in conflict for centuries and that's why laws are in place to settle their differences. Then the Prime Minister announces that there'll be no evictions for a month. What does that mean in action, I wonder? If someone doesn't pay his/her rent for a month, he/she won't be evicted during that month, but will have to pay double rent the following month? And if she/he doesn't pay it, she/he will be evicted at some later stage? And the 'where' and 'how' of housing homeless people is yet another confusing issue regarding accommodation, since the recent increase is said to be related to people losing their jobs. Whether the governments' statements made are off-the-cuff or representative of hours of forethought, they might seem superficially appealing but are proving meaningless.

7. We've had decades of a movement by employers – including government employers – towards casualisation of the workforce (along with fancy language such as 'gig economy', 'freedom to choose employment options', and 'independent contracting') as the security of full-time permanent jobs disappeared for so many. Now the pay claims made by 'jobkeepers' and 'jobseekers' alike are being refused by Centrelink, often because they've worked for a series of different employers as part-timers or casuals over the past 12 months rather than working for a single employer. And the reason that's the case is that small business employers weren't able to afford to offer them longer-term employment.

8. Finally, I've heard today that someone who has worked as a casual swimming teacher, with full-time hours, at a local council pool for a decade is not eligible for Jobkeeper payments – based on the percentage drop in profitability of that profit-centre, the Council swimming pool. When I say, 'someone', I mean all those employees who have been employed as casuals over the long and short term by councils and semi-government employers. Whichever government ministers are responsible for setting the guidelines – by which staff at Centrelink judge a worker eligible or ineligible for

payments – should either fix the guidelines or resign.

How muddled is my thinking? How muddled is yours?

I'm very much in favour of strict social policies for a lockdown to reduce the effects of coronavirus. But what we're witnessing every day on 'breaking news' is leadership gone haywire and policy on the run.

I'm wondering … if these are my views from inside my genteel hotel accommodation, will they change when I see the light of day on the outside next week?

Part 8
Feeling rather house proud today

(or should I say 'fière de ma chambre'?) ... I've easily been able to carry out my simple laundry and washing up chores, as well as think 'neat', with my bits & bobs all in their proper places. This internment does stretch on, though.

Can you imagine what it would be like in a real internment camp for refugees? I can't. With no definite end in sight. Would it be a thousand times worse than this lock-up? Oh, so much more than that ...

Here I can look forward to release on Monday, and in the meantime gaze out on the city street traffic (not much of that these days), appreciate the rain, and view a few balconies and deciduous trees which will begin to lose their leaves soon. A good thing I'm here now and not later in the season.

After resisting bedroom activity of all kinds except sleep for a week, this morning I went down on my knees, onto my carpeted floor, to do some exercises. Once you form the habit, it becomes easier, I told a friend yesterday to encourage her. So now I feel I have to follow my own advice.

Using a loose combination of yoga and physio stretches, I warn myself that I mustn't be too vigorous in case I pull a muscle. Well, I'm sure we're all aware there's very little chance of that, considering my level of exertion. A friend has recommended a video by The Australian Ballet's Artistic Director, David McAllister, 'How to do a plié'. It's delightful! https://www.youtube.com/watch?v=3eOEdjLtLKk

I must admit, though, my favourite exercise for my upper back comes from physiotherapist, Kam Barbhra, from Lilyfield Physiotherapy. It's so energising, and extremely demanding of focus, but not at all boisterous. The instructions:
Take a bath towel.
Roll it lengthwise.
Place it on the floor.
Lie down on your back along its length so that your spine feels the support, and let your shoulders fall back.
Breathe deeply!

I recommend it! And you can stay there as long as you like … (but take care you don't fall asleep). Yes, you can try it at home as long as you don't ever tell who advised you.

Here are another couple of stress relief recommendations for anyone who likes children:

https://www.youtube.com/watch?v=YTaUc6H9aPg

& Sophie Fatu

https://www.youtube.com/watch?v=Ot64V57qJcE

Part 9
As one of the travellers from Peru quarantined ...

In a Sydney hotel since March 31 – and due to emerge into the 'real world' this coming Monday – I'm pleased to know that, as I write, another party of 280 Australians is on its way back home from Peru on a Qantas flight to Melbourne.

It's taking a while, but at last the government is involved in flights being organised from several places, some as distant as Nepal, with fares reduced and loans available for those who can't afford the fares up front.

It's so easy in life to grumble – and so difficult at times to see the value of life in micro.

But what a wonderful discovery I've made here in my hotel room, to find a true soul mate! Perhaps even a great love, even though he's quite old and dessicated. *I can handle that*, I think as I hop up into bed, wrapping my silk scarf around my shoulders for warmth.

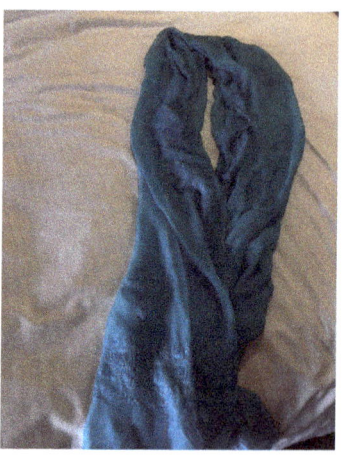

In any case, aware as you must be by now of my proclivity for French culture, imagine my curiosity when a friend living in Seattle*, who read my blog recently, suggested I check out, *Voyage Around My Room*, written by Count Xavier de Maistre.

Sure, I've heard about this book, somewhere in my dark past … but to rediscover it in this setting – confined as I am to a room with a bed, a sofa and a table (plus a bathroom and kitchenette, I admit, though they're not relevant to this matter of coincidence) – has created *un resonance exquisite*. Seriously. Please stay with me on a journey around my room …

I found the book on Google and was able to open it in part, to quickly develop a taste for the author's arch yet confident style and purely optimistic tone.

Former editor of *The Paris Review*, Richard Howard explains in the Introduction that in 1790, de Maistre, a 27-year-old Savoyard officer stationed in Turin, was punished for fighting a duel and put under house arrest for 42 days, during which time he wrote a text 'to beguile the languors of his solitude'.

Now I ask you, isn't that what I've been trying to do, 'beguile the languors of my solitude'? And mostly achieving it with the help of meditation, a few exercises, and my impulse to share the experience with you, dear readers. Although I do confess I stayed in bed longer than usual this morning simply because I'd woken at 3 am. That jetlag is a surprise package, isn't it?

Howard goes on to write that four years after writing *Voyage autour de ma chambre*, de Maistre left the manuscript in Lausanne with his older brother Joseph, who published it the following year without his brother's knowledge.

'Two centuries later we are astonished by the many anomalies which these circumstances present to current notions of authorship, of intellectuality,' Howard writes.

'Our amazement at the oddities of the young count's career,' as Howard describes it, are enhanced by the discovery that he flew in a hot-air balloon made by the brothers Montgolfier. De Maistre's brother advised against publishing a sequel, *Expedition nocturne autour de ma chambre,* as 'according to the Spanish proverb, Part II is always bad'. The work remained in manuscript until 1825, four years after Joseph's death, when it was published in Paris to considerable success.

According to Howard, 'The texts have been accorded a certain classical, or academic, success; they are *récits*, a genre which has long been appreciated in France (from Constant to Camus, with brilliant illustrations by Gide and Blanchot) and exemplified as well in Russia (*Notes from Underground*, for example) in Italy, and of course in England, where the personal essay invariably threatens to spill over into this protean form. A *récit* is a sort of dramatic monologue in prose concerned with the problematics of narrative, questioning the nature of such pronouns as 'I', 'he', and 'you', and given … to notions of literature as process rather than as product. De Maistre's versions are among the liveliest and the most lenient in the repertoire.'

And so we proceed to an excerpt from de Maistre's work (with my square brackets inserted without apology):

'I will no longer keep my book *in petto* – here it is, gentlemen [and women]. Read it. I have just competed a forty-two-day voyage around my room. The fascinating observations I made and the endless pleasures I experienced along the way made me wish to share my travels with the public; and the certainty of having something useful to offer convinced me to do so. Words cannot describe the satisfaction I feel in my heart when I think of the infinite number of unhappy souls for whom I am providing a sure antidote to boredom and a palliative to their ills. For the pleasure of traveling around one's room is beyond the reach of man's restless jealousy: it depends not on one's material circumstance. …

My room ... runs from east to west, and forms a rectangle that is thirty-six paces around, keeping well nigh to the walls. My voyage, however, will encompass a great deal more; for I shall often walk across it lengthwise and breadthwise, and diagonally too, following no rule or method. ... My soul is so open to every manner of idea, taste and sentiment, it avidly takes in everything that turns up. ... I too, when traveling in my room, rarely follow a straight line! I go from my table toward a painting hung in a corner, and from there I set off obliquely for the door; yet although in setting out my intention is to reach that spot, if I happen to encounter my armchair along the way, without hesitation I settle right down into it. What a splendid piece of furniture an armchair is, of utmost importance and usefulness for every contemplative man [and woman!]. During those long winter evenings, it is often sweet and always advisable to stretch out luxuriously in one, far from the din of the crowds. A good fire, a few books, a few quills – what excellent antidotes to boredom! And what a pleasure then to forget your books and quills and to poke the fire, relinquishing your thoughts to some pleasant meditation – or composing some rhymes to amuse your friends: the hours slide over you and fall silently into eternity, and you do not even feel their melancholy passing.'

Isn't the writing and intention just so elegant, so leisured and so appreciative of the nature of the mind, and the small pleasures of life? And thrilling for me that my room too 'runs from east to west', I walk it 'lengthwise and breadthwise', my soul is 'open to [almost] every manner of idea, taste [but not carnivorous] and sentiment [plenty of that supplied by the current coronavirus crisis], and what a 'splendid piece of furniture' my sofa is (in the absence of an armchair). No matter that I don't have quills - I have a mobile and the internet to hand, to create my blogs for you, reader, out of the thin air of this room. *Absolument charmant* is de Maistre's approach!

Absolument charmant! As in the kind of bedroom that Google gives us to demonstrate the expression, which I agree is nothing like de Maistre's room nor my hotel room. But I did ask you to stay with me on this short journey in synchronicity. And at least I've supplied a pretty picture.

Oh, and I forgot to say that one of the two books I have with me is about prose poetry … indefinable yet so close in purpose to *recit*, linking personal sentiment and simplicity of materiality.

Wait! Attends, *s'il te plait*. Do you think it might be possible that my French *poesie* et culture approach is perhaps becoming just a little obsessive, getting the upper hand in this small hotel room? You can tell me. Not long to go until I escape.

* My Seattle friend Dr Rebecca Cummins, an artist and University of Washington Professor, points out that 'Voyage autour de ma chambre' is enjoying a resurrection in these times - as another alternative to Camus' 'The Plague'.

Part 10
Ooh-la-la Easter Monday

How fresh the air, how scenic the landscape, how free my spirit feels.

Am I lost for words? Almost but not quite. So I'll use this final blog about being quarantined to celebrate life itself – our blessed lives – even within the restrictions of self-isolation that most people in the world are now experiencing to greater or lesser degree, or soon will be. To celebrate each other, to celebrate those who are dedicated to caring for others, and to honour life in the face of death for so many.

Following on from my last blog in which I was quite overcome by the literary charms of a French writer, I want to reflect here on another French novelist, Georges Perec, who may be considered to have had an impact on global writing to rival that of de Maistre.

Perec's best-known novel, Life A User's Manual, or in the original La Vie mode d'emploi, comprises many stories about residents of an apartment block in Paris, told from alternating perspectives. So much of Perec's novel and essay writing involves experimental wordplay and lists and, coloured by melancholy, inevitably raises questions of identity. Perec encouraged looking at the familiar, whether that be the space of the home or the larger world. Questions of where home is, and what it means, which go beyond its monetary value, point towards a major question facing many in the 21st century: nationalism vs globalisation.

Similarly, in 12 Edmondstone Street, Australian writer David Malouf explored how geography and its landmarks form our sense of self. 'Malouf begins by describing, in loving, evocative detail, the house in which he was born and grew up in Brisbane, moving from room to room, always relating the smallest items in it to the life he remembers and his widening perception of the world at large.'

But this blog is not primarily a guide to stories about familiar rooms and foreign countries but more a reflection on how we view ourselves within a confined and unfamiliar space, namely a hotel room that you can't get out of. Until you can. Until you're given permission by the police after a health check and then a wrist tag. And since my liberation this morning, I now view my identity in a reversal of perspective as being about small mercies and graces, rather than small spaces. And specifically, to remember the role they play in my life. Not just giving them a tick – 'Yes, I feel grateful that I'm alive, da-dum,' but 'It's a tiny miracle within a great universe that I was born, lived a happy childhood and then so long as an adult, given the global odds of any individual being born into such a benign culture and economy – and most of this has not been my own achievement but gained through the small mercies and graces shown by so many others towards me'.

It's still the case today – here in a society where the great majority of people have agreed to the emphatic carrot-and-stick self-isolation proposal by our freely elected leaders – for virtually all of us, except those in essential services, to recognise the need to close down business and stay in our homes for an indefinite period. Sure, most people are angry about one aspect or another: e.g. all share fear of death; many, physical restriction; scarcity of food; lack of an income. But we've all agreed that we have no choice if we're to weather this coronavirus storm with as few lives lost as possible. By the grace and mercy not necessarily of a 'God' – for those who may not believe in that concept – but by mutual support and cooperation, the humanist understanding in the lyrics, 'We're all in this together'. And those at the forefront in caring for coronavirus patients – health workers, cleaners and waste collectors – are the bravest and most honoured among us. We owe them so much.

Both dangers and opportunities can arise in life, and I feel fortunate that the timing turned out to be exquisitely, finely tempered for my travel and its repercussions: to leave Australia before advice was given not to travel overseas; to experience the birth of a grandson in Peru; to go into lockdown there before finding a flight back home; to book and pay for the ticket before being told I'd be safe in compulsory quarantine for 14 days; and to be so relieved to have the chance to be in my home place again.

Yes, from my viewpoint today, the unintended adventure, as it evolved, was experienced by me as if I was a disembodied particle of energy driven by love – on a journey made up of many small mercies and graces by people on two continents either side of the Pacific Ocean, and in a metal tube being flown there and back, across that vast sea. It was the least I could do to put up with a comfortable though confined room for a fortnight, without being able to step out into the corridor … and I kept reminding myself of that.

So how long will I remember the good fortune? As long as I can appreciate the world around me (hotel den or open space) and not have my thoughts overtaken by an incessant inner voice. As Krishnamurti advises, 'the word is not the thing'. The word 'tree' is not a tree. Nor is a photo, which is merely a reminder of the actual. A tree is the living being which is nurtured by the earth – just as we are. Our true home is hewn in nature's space of animals, plants, and clean air and water.

After all, we're all made of the same stuff – predominantly hydrogen, and in the animal world, heart, mind, breath – with just a touch or a flourish of one tint or tone different in each one of us.

And with that riff on identity, travel, enclosure and freedom, I'll bid you au revoir – until we meet again soon online.

All packed up - including laundry ...

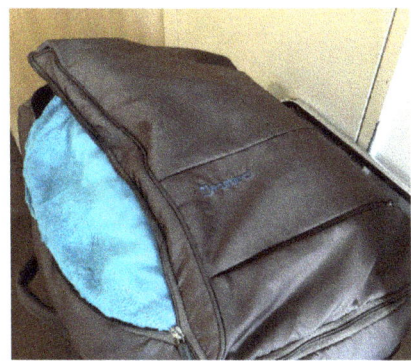
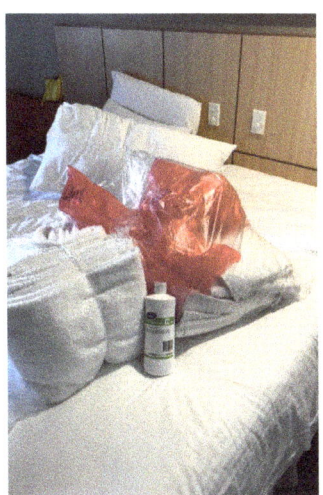

wristband donned …

... and police protection ended.

1. 'Life A User's Manual' Georges Perec, Hachette Livre Paris (1978).
2. Review of David Malouf memoir-novel, '12 Edmondstone Street' Penguin (1985) from http://australian-cultural-atlas.info/CAA/listing.php?id=46 .
3. 'We're all in this together' – Matthew Gerrard; Robbie Nevil, (2006).
4. 'I Am Australian' (1987) song lyrics – Bruce Woodley (The Seekers) & Dobe Newton (The Bushwackers).

www.ingramcontent.com/pod-product-compliance
Ingram Content Group UK Ltd.
Pitfield, Milton Keynes, MK11 3LW, UK
UKHW022119230426
12048UKWH00010BA/597